7 YEARS FR

BOOKS BY PHILIP LEVINE

7 Years from Somewhere　　1979

Ashes: Poems Old and New　　1979

The Names of the Lost　　1976

1933　　1974

They Feed They Lion　　1972

Red Dust　　1971

Pili's Wall　　1971

Not This Pig　　1968

On the Edge　　1963

7 Years from
Somewhere

POEMS BY
PHILIP LEVINE

NEW YORK ATHENEUM 1979

My thanks to the National Endowment for the Arts from which I received a grant that gave me the free time to write many of these poems.

My thanks to the editors of the following magazines in which these poems first appeared:

THE AMERICAN POETRY REVIEW *(Hear Me)*
ANTAEUS *(Andorra, You Can Have It, 7 Years from Somewhere)*
ANTIOCH REVIEW *(Words)*
BERKELEY POETRY REVIEW *(Toward Home)*
FIELD *(I Could Believe, Left on the Shore, Planting, Milkweed, Dark Head, Little by Little)*
HARPER'S *(Francisco, I'll Bring You Red Carnations)*
INQUIRY *(Each Time is Different)*
IOWA REVIEW *(Ricky, Let Me Be)*
MISSOURI REVIEW *(Your Life)*
NEW LEADER *(Now it can be Told)*
NEW LETTERS *(Asking)*
THE NEW YORKER *(The Life Ahead, The Gift, The Last Step, The Face, Let Me Begin Again, One for the Rose, Snow, Dawn—1952)*
THE OHIO REVIEW *(In the Dark)*
POETRY *(Here and Now)*
QUARTERLY WEST *(Peace)*

My special thanks to my friends Peter Everwine, Fran Levine, Larry Levis, Ada Long, Stan Plumly, David St. John, and Charles Wright, some of whom endured this book over and over and all of whom insisted on changes and deletions in the face of spirited resistance.

Library of Congress Cataloging in Publication Data

Levine, Philip, 1928-
    Seven years from somewhere.

    I. Title.
PS3562.E9S4 1979   811'.5'4   78-20595
ISBN 0-689-10974-1

This book is for you

CONTENTS

I

I COULD BELIEVE

I could come to believe
almost anything, even
my soul, which is
my unlit cigar, even
the earth that huddled
all these years to
my bones, waiting
for the little of me
it would claim. I
could believe my sons
would grow into
tall lean booted men
driving cattle trucks
to Monday markets,
and my mother would
climb into the stars
hand over hand,
a woman of imagination
and stamina among
the airy spaces
of broken clouds,
and I, middle aged
and heavy, would
buy my suits by
the dozen, vested ones,
and wear a watch chain
stretched across my
middle. Even with none
of that, alone, and
naked at the club,
laid out to be rubbed
down, I would groan
orders to a T-shirted
half wit. I came
home from Spain, bitter
and wounded, opened
a small portrait shop

in an office building
in Detroit, hired
an alcoholic camera man
and married a homely woman
good with books. It is
1943 and young girls
wait in line for
the white lights blinding
them, drop their blouses
and shoulder straps
and smile for the men
scrambling on Pacific
atolls. I have bought
a second shop
on Washington Blvd.
When I can't stand it
I drive out past the lights
of the small factories
where the bearings for tanks
and half-tracks are ground,
and park and smoke
in silence on the shoulder
of US 24, 7000 miles
from my lost Spain,
a lifetime from the Ebro
where 7 men I came to need
went under in a small boat
and I crossed alone
to a burnt shore and kept
running. Someone said
it was Prospect Park
in the summer, except
for the dying. Except
for the dying this
would be heaven and I,
37 years old, would be
a man I could talk to

or a body fallen away
to the dust of Spain,
a white face becoming
water, a name no one
names, a scramble
of sounds, hiccups
and the striking of teeth
against teeth, except
for the dying I
would be dead, my face
born forever on an
inside page of the Detroit
Free Press, except
for the dying I could
believe.

LEFT ON THE SHORE

One small hat
the shore birds prayed in,
two beached stars that pointed
the way of the wind,
three egg-shells that held
three sullen planets.
I came upon all this
in the first of middle age
and passed right by
so wise had I grown
in the forty years that turned
my head gray and my
feet flat, so full was I
of schemes for making water
out of ordinary seas
and something of myself.
The wind blew down
my shirt and up my pants,
the sea raged and boiled,
it was late in the year,
too late to be out for fun.
And there I was, going
nowhere and seeing nothing
while the birds bowed their heads
all at one time
and two hands told the wind
where and how hard
and the earth and its pale sisters
looked upon everything
for the first and the last time.

PEACE

Our words go slowly out
and the sun burns
them before they
can speak. It is
as though the earth
were tired of our talk
and wanted peace, an end
to promises, perhaps
an end to us. And we
merely turn to a window
and gaze upon the farmer
and his horse slowly
plowing the field they
plowed the day before.
The sun has risen
and within an hour
it will begin to drop
and in the lengthening
shadows a known cold
will waken and step
towards us. You will
touch my shoulder
just once, and I will
close the window
and turn to see your
eyes, bright and alive,
your mouth holding
a smile as best
it can. There is still
light upon your broad
forehead I have seen
bathed in sweat, light
upon cheeks and chin,
and now that light is
going too. No one
said it would be easy.

ANDORRA

Someone was burning wood
a mile off, and the blue smoke
rose in the late November air.
Below me the stream rushed
over small stones, and I stared
to the bottom, feeling the cold
though I stood in the day's first
sunlight entering this high valley.
The day will be short. In 5 hours
the sun will drop below the mountains.
The cold will rise from damp stones
and the racing waters. Would I have
stood silently blessing each grain,
speckled and stained, if I had known
that in one corner of my heart
a wound was spreading to fill
my throat with the bitter tastes
of someone else? The man I was
smiles into the light, young
and full of hope. He will leave
the bridge and lean down to splash
the freezing water on his face
and shake his head as though he
were saying No! No! to everything.
He is wakening to a day as pure
as new snow, a day like no
other, cold and black at the edges
and elusive as light at the center,
a day on which he will climb
high above the village and sing
in his cracked voice to everyone
and no one. A man alone, ignorant,
strong, holding the burning moments
for all they're worth. Turning now
in my memory to climb higher
and higher until he is only a small
moving dot among great gray mounds,

and then is out of sight. Across
the valley smoke twists blue
and dream-like into the last light.

PLANTING

A soldier runs home
and finds his mother has turned
to iron and the pots are gone.
He finds a small note
from the mice—they took
the silver and won't be back.
How can he return, how
can he march to war
knowing his mother may fall
from the clouds or before that
he may begin to laugh
at nothing and go on laughing
until he grows as tall
as the wayside trees.
He knows he is hungry
and alone. War will do nothing
for him. He knows
each house has gathered
its stories of dust and hurt
and waits under the sycamores
for fire to free it. He knows
it is foolish to be marching
away as long as one cloud
carries the sea back to land.
So he writes a letter
to the year and explains
how he was meant to make
something else, a ball
of earth out of his ears
or music from his wishbone
or a perfect watercolor
from the sparrow's tears, he
was meant to grow small
and still, a window
on the world, a map
that can show him home.
He goes out to the fields

and plants it word by word,
hurling it into the wind
and feels it come back, soft,
burning, heavy with rain.

THE LIFE AHEAD

I wakened, still a child,
and dressed myself slowly
for the life ahead. It
came at two, after lunch,
the class quieted
and the teacher's eyes
clouded and closed.
I could smell our coats
on their hooks, I could
smell my own uncut hair,
the hair of a dog, and
when I looked down below
to the dark streets awash
with oil, a small boy—
alone and lost—wandered
across the playground.
He climbed the fence
and made it across
the avenue, past the closed
candy store, and down
the street that led to hell.
There was a river in Detroit
and if you crossed it you
were in another country,
but something always
called me back, a woman
who had no use for me
or a brother who did, or
the pure white aura
of steel before the forge
came down with a groan
like the sea's and we stood
back waiting for one more
leaf of a truck spring, thick
arched leaf of earth. Something
called me back to this life,
and I came home to wander

the schoolyard again
as a lost boy and find
above or below the world
was here and now, drowning
in oil, second by second
borrowed from the clock.

RICKY

I go into the back yard
and arrange some twigs
and a few flowers. I go alone
and speak to you as I never could
when you lived, when you
smiled back at me shyly.
Now I can talk to you as I talked
to a star when I was a boy,
expecting no answer, as I talked
to my father who had become
the wind, particles of rain
and fire, these few twigs
and flowers that have no name.

———

Last night they said a rosary
and my boys went, awkward
in slacks and sport shirts,
and later sitting under the hidden
stars they were attacked and beaten.
You are dead. It is 105,
the young and the old burn
in the fields, and though they cry
enough the sun hangs on
bloodying the dust above the aisles
of cotton and grape.

———

This morning they will say a mass
and then the mile-long line of cars.
Teddy and John, their faces swollen,
and four others will let you
slowly down into the fresh earth
where you go on. Scared now,
they will understand some of it.
Not the mass or the rosary
or the funeral, but the rage.
Not you falling through the dark,
moving underwater like a flower
no one could find until
it was too late and you had gone out,
your breath passing through dark water
never to return to the young man,
pigeon-breasted, who rode
his brother's Harley up the driveway.

—————

Wet grass sticks to my feet, bright
marigold and daisy burst in the new day.
The bees move at the clumps
of clover, the carrots—
almost as tall as I—
have flowered, pale lacework.
Hard dark buds
of next year's oranges, new green
of slick leaves, yellow grass
tall and blowing by the fence. The grapes
are slow, climbing the arbor,
but some day there will be shade
here where the morning sun whitens
everything and punishes my eyes.

—————

Your people worked
for some small piece of earth,
for a home, adding a room
a boy might want. Butchie said
you could have the Harley
if only you would come back,
anything that was his.
A dog barks down the block
and it is another day. I hear
the soft call of the dove,
screech of mockingbird and jay.
A small dog picks up the tune,
and then *tow-weet tow-weet*
of hidden birds, and two finches
darting over the low trees—
there is no end.

———

What can I say to this mound
of twigs and dry flowers, what
can I say now that I would speak
to you? Ask the wind, ask
the absence or the rose burned
at the edges and still blood red.
And the answer is you
falling through black water
into the stillness that fathers
the moon, the bees ramming into
the soft cups, the eucalyptus
swaying like grass under water.
My John told me your cousin
punched holes in the wall
the night you died and was afraid
to be alone. Your brother
walks staring at the earth.
I am afraid of water.

———

And the earth goes on
in blinding sunlight.
I hold your image
a moment, the long
Indian face
the brown almond eyes
your dark skin full
and glowing as you grew
into the hard body
of a young man.

And now it is bird screech
and a tree rat suddenly
parting the tall grass
by the fence, lumbering
off, and in the distance
the crashing of waves
against some shore
maybe only in memory.

We lived by the sea.
My boys wrote
postcards and missed you
and your brother. I slept
and wakened to the sea,
I remember in my dreams
water pounded the windows
and walls, it seeped
through everything,
and like your spirit,
like your breath,
nothing could contain it.

FRANCISCO, I'LL BRING YOU RED CARNATIONS

Here in the great cemetery
behind the fortress of Barcelona
I have come once more to see
the graves of my fallen.
Two ancient picnickers direct
us down the hill "Durruti,"
says the man, "I was on
his side." The woman hushes
him. All the way down
this is a city of the dead,
871,251 *difuntos*.
The poor packed in tenements
a dozen high; the rich
in splendid homes or temples.
So nothing has changed
except for the single
unswerving fact: they are
all dead. Here is the Plaza
of San Jaime, here the Rambla
of San Pedro, so every death
still has a mailing address,
but since this is Spain
the mail never comes or
comes too late to be of use.
Between the cemetery and
the Protestant burial ground
we find the three stones
all in a row: Ferrer Guardia,
B. Durruti, F. Ascaso, the names
written with marking pens,
and a few circled A's and tributes
to the FAI and CNT.
For two there are floral
displays, but Ascaso faces
eternity with only a stone.
Maybe as it should be. He was
a stone, a stone and a blade,

the first grinding and sharpening
the other. Half his 36
years were spent in prisons
or on the run, and yet
in that last photograph
taken less than an hour before
he died, he stands in a dark
suit, smoking, a rifle slung
behind his shoulder, and glances
sideways at the camera
half smiling. It is July 20,
1936, and before the darkness
falls a darkness will have
fallen on him. While
the streets are echoing
with victory and revolution,
Francisco Ascaso will take up
the hammered little blade
of his spirit and enter for
the last time the republics
of death. I remember
his words to a frightened
comrade who questioned
the wisdom of attack: "We
have gathered here to die, but we
don't have to die with dogs,
so go." Forty-one years
ago, and now the city stretches
as far as the eye can see,
huge cement columns like nails
pounded into the once green
meadows of the Llobregat.
Your Barcelona is gone,
the old town swallowed
in industrial filth and
the burning mists of gasoline.
Only the police remain, armed

and arrogant, smiling masters
of the boulevards, the police
and your dream of the city
of God, where every man
and every woman gives
and receives the gifts of work
and care, and that dream
goes on in spite of slums,
in spite of death clouds,
the roar of trucks, the harbor
staining the mother sea,
it goes on in spite of all
that mocks it. We have it here
growing in our hearts, as
your comrade said, and when
we give it up with our last
breaths someone will gasp
it home to their lives.
Francisco, stone, knife blade,
single soldier still on
the run down the darkest
street of all, we will be back
across an ocean and a continent
to bring you red carnations,
to celebrate the unbroken
promise of your life that
once was frail and flesh.

HERE AND NOW

The waters of earth come and go
like the waters of this sea
broken as it is out of the dust
of other men. Don't ask me why
I came down to the water's edge—
hell, I was young, and I thought
I knew life, I thought I could
hold the darkness the way a man
holds a cup of coffee before
he wakens, the way he pulls
at a cigarette and wonders
how he came to this room, the walls
scarred with the gray brush
of years, how he travelled so long
to waken this sagging bed, and takes
up his gray socks one by one
and the heavy shoes smelling of oil,
and doesn't cry out or even sigh
for fear he will hear. So I stood
and let the waves climb up
the dark shore. The village
slept behind me, my wife,
my kids, still dreaming of home,
and I, the dog of the house,
prowled the darkened streets
which led here and to silence,
the first cold light smearing
the eastern sky and the Levante
blowing its warm salt breath
in my face. If I had commanded
the sun to stand still the day
would have come on moment
by moment climbing the white walls
of the town, if I'd cursed the air
it would've lightened before
my eyes, at last a fire
at the tip of each wave, and in

its depths the sea turning from gray
to a dense blue. So I said
nothing, but when my eyes filled
slowly with the first salted
rains of sorrow, I let them
come believing I wept for joy
at the gift of one more day.
I suppose the wind still blows
at ease across the sleeping face
of the village I fled all those years
ago, and some young man comes
down to the sea and murmers a word,
his name, or God's, or a child's,
or maybe just the sea's. Let him
be wiser than I, let him fight back
the tears and taste only the sea's salt,
let him take what he can—
the trembling of his hands,
the silence before him, the slow
awakening of his eyes, the windows
of the town opening on first light,
the children starting suddenly
from their twisted sheets with a cry
of neither victory or defeat,
only the surprise of having come back
to what no one promised, here and now.

MILKWEED

Remember how unimportant
they seemed, growing loosely
in the open fields we crossed
on the way to school. We
would carve wooden swords
and slash at the lucious trunks
until the white milk started
and then flowed. Then we'd
go on to the long day after
day of the History of History
or the tables of numbers and order
as the clock slowly paid
out the moments. The windows
went dark first with rain
and then snow, and then the days,
then the years ran together and not
one mattered more than
another, and not one mattered.

Two days ago I walked
the empty woods, bent over,
crunching through oak leaves,
asking myself questions
without answers. From somewhere
a froth of seeds drifted by touched
with gold in the last light
of a lost day, going with
the wind as they always did.

II

THE GIFT

Wheat fields the wind praised
and the great river freighted
with long barges of logs
and then on past the darkening
fields where suddenly a town
sprouted, tall silos, loading docks,
and a long train chuffing
toward the night. I went on,
farther and farther from home,
toward where the mountains lifted
me, slowly at first, then
suddenly the dark steep climbs
and here and there a pair
of eyes burning like tiny candles
by the roadside. At last, dawn
broke behind me. I pulled
over and slept an hour or two
and woke at a great height,
turning above the frozen earth
as though I were a bird
or had woken from dreaming
into dreaming. But this was
me, different now, or so
I thought, still a man, still
lonely even at great height,
but remembering it all, the city
where I thought I'd died,
the river black at night
with darkness or with oil
or both, gleaming with the lights
of all the fires that burned
beside it. I was still there
even if that had passed, even
if all the lives that held me
let me go and then themselves
let go. I could return
some day and walk the same streets

in the same light and no one
would look my way or say my name.
I was there because I had
to be, but this flying in paled air,
breathing of fallen crystals
and blank stone above the tree line,
this soaring without wings
and without faith, this was
the world no one promised me.

YOUR LIFE

I did not know your life
was mine. I had seen you
walking sadly by, your head
down, your hands still and hidden,
and I thought, I could go to you
and ask what the years had done
that couldn't be forgotten.
Instead I turned inward. I found
the long still hours of silence
that were childhood. Once
my aunt went away at dawn,
and I sat in an empty house
until the front windows darkened
and I fell asleep. That boy
never wakened. The one who did
was tall and stronger than I
am now, and he spoke to no one.
He smoked, spit, drove with his eyes
closed, and by himself he built
the road from Gary to Hammond.
That was thirty years ago, when
a single man was something.
Now I will turn outward, to
the little clearing in the woods
where you at last have kneeled
to find the earth is all the home
you need. I am beside you—
feel the warm air at your ear.
It's not the dreaded land wind
or the word of God. It's the breath
of one man, a man like any other,
fallen to this earth, as all men
have, to say, Your life is mine.

TOWARD HOME

The years are turning
toward home, and I
am entering the forest
of no trees, the winds
that bring neither heat
or rain. No bigger
than the stone you kicked
out of your way, still
I am all there is
of someone who lived
beside the great sea
and listened to its prayers.
Do you remember how
once you took my hand
and led me to a white room
I'd never seen before?
You held me close and said
my name again and again,
although the name was
wrong, the name of someone
I never was. Do you
recall that night? I was
awake even before the light
had moved from between
the leafless trees
and entered the dusty window
and touched your face open
beside me. How long ago
was it? I slipped out
from between the clean sheets
and stood naked and cold
on the bare wood floor
sorting my clothes from yours,
needing to return to a life
that was no more me
than any other life,
to a room I paid for

and so could say was mine,
to a blue work shirt softened
with use and bearing a name
that also was not mine.
In the mirror I saw
a body, mine, thickened
with years of work but still
soft and shadowed in those
small valleys where so few
hands had strayed, a body
you said had grown precious
in its deformities. Even
then, combing my tangled hair
with the hardened fingers
with which I stained
the world, I inhaled
the perfume of our sweat
and thought, No one
will ever shape my face
so perfectly or hold
so much of me in her eyes
and name it all. And no one
ever has. All those years
ago, I walked in the frozen
January air, chanting
my happiness to no one
along the curving road
that led toward town,
that led toward manhood,
toward you again and again,
toward age, madness, this
coming to be the salt
the sea would crust
over the eyelids of
my closed face, toward
the pebble washed ashore,
the moon that turned

its face away, toward
everything for which there
were no names, no open hands,
no voice to even try.

ASKING

Once, in the beginning
on the last Sunday
of a lost August,
I sat on the Canadian shore
of Lake Huron and watched
the dark clouds go over,
knowing this was the end
of summer. There was a girl
beside me, but we
barely knew each other,
and so we sat
in our separate thoughts,
or I did anyway. I saw
how it would be, summer
after summer, working
toward a few days like this
when I came flushed
with strength and money,
my hands scarred
and hardened, my shoulders
and arms thick, and maybe
I would find a girl
or maybe I'd get drunk
and fight or growing older
just get drunk and sit
alone staring into a glass
the way my uncles did.
When I felt the girl's hand
on the back of my neck
I shuddered the way you do
when a cool wind
passes over you, and she
misunderstood and pulled
her hand away. I took
her hand in mine and said
something about having
drifted off and how odd

it was to know a season
had ended at one moment
and I had turned
toward winter, maybe
a lifetime of winters.
Then I thought of her
working week after week
in the office
of a small contractor
she said she hated
and going home to the father
she said she hated
and the mother who went on
about marriage and was
she ever going to get out,
and she just barely 22.
Almost 30 years ago.
She and I never saw
each other after we
got back to Detroit
in the smoky light
of early evening.
I let her out
a block from her house
and said I'd call her,
but knew I wouldn't
knowing what I did
about her life and how
she needed someone
I wasn't. I went back
to my room and sat
in the dark wondering
how can I get out.
I knew there must be
millions of us,
alone and frightened,
feeling the sudden chill

of winter, of time
gathering and falling
like a shadow across
our lives. Wondering
what was the answer.
Only a boy, still alone,
still solemn, turning
in the darkness
toward manhood, turning
as the years turned
imperceptibly, petal
by petal, closing
for the night,
the question still
unanswered, that question
never to be asked again.

HEAR ME

I watch the filthy light seep through
the cracked shutters and stain the walls
of this third-rate hotel, and I rise
and go downstairs to walk among
the bodies of the lost men who have
come to die in Barcelona. They are
so small, each a tiny pale planet
whirring slowly toward that burning
each of us will embrace. Open-mouthed
they sigh in the damp morning. Bread
will not save them—holy bread,
common bread, conquered bread, no
bread will save them. Wine they have,
their lips and chins are darkened,
and that didn't save them. If God
cared he would send an old crone
to waken each of them and whisper
that in work is salvation, and
there would be great laughter,
for they have become work.
That one who is still only a boy
is first the ringing of a hammer
on steel. If you put your ear
to his chest you will hear the music
of salvation breaking his heart.
The old one wiping this morning
from his forehead with a soiled cap
was born in a house with a well.
He ate the well, and the four walls,
and the fireless nights that crushed
his hopes. He wants a cigarette.
His work is eating, and before dusk
has climbed the walls of this plaza
he will have eaten the rage
of all our lungs. The others,
why have they come from all
the small places to this place

if not to find the crone hidden
in an English raincoat. The crone
who will not say "conquer your bread"
because I have spit out that lie.
Who will not say, "Take this wine"
because I took it and I am drunk.
Who will not say "work" because I
know that never worked. You,
sitting alone, put your ear
to my chest or take this damp head
motherless from birth and smother
me against the hardened body
of all you've lost, and hear me,
hear me praying to die in Barcelona.

LITTLE BY LITTLE

Each year I tire a little more.
In the impossible dawn
of August the last cool
of night air sighs. There goes out
from me a groan that stops
the mockingbird in mid-squawk.
This will be the last year,
it says, but I know otherwise.
I know the price I pay
simply to be. I have stood
by the shore and watched
the old men sail out
in darkness, and I turned
for home and a tiny bed.
I slept while they saw
dawn flood each others' faces.
Later, I woke and dressed
one foot at a time, brushed,
and went down to the wharf
to buy what I could. They stood
to one side, silent, smoking,
and still slowly rocking
on the great pulse of ocean.
Men with the faces of time
and the bodies of boys,
they sat now, legs apart, barefoot,
their waists cinched by old ropes,
and nodded closer and closer to sleep.
They would die all at once,
in a tangle of sails and black
rushing overhead, they would
go out like candles suddenly
sucked up, while I gave up
a finger one day, a tooth the next,
an ear and all it heard,
a few hairs that moved the wind,
an eye that made the hills rise

in morning light. I would give up
first your hand that rested
on the back of mine, then
the glass of water between us,
the table where you sewed
and I read. Finally, each word
you spoke, and each shrug,
our coughs, our names,
our tongues, our questions
and even the silence that dusted
our eyelids as the answer,
or rained in the streets at night
while the sky bulked larger
and darker toward morning.

IN THE DARK

I.

Each hour of this life
I see the darkness
more clearly, see how
it lives in the shadows
of the wild phlox, how
it climbs the valley ash
at dusk and finally crowns
the leaves, how it rises
then slowly from the grass.
The trees are still. I
hold my breath that one
moment and suddenly
tiny fires blur the sky
but cannot make it light.

2.

The woman who sleeps
beside me is dreaming
of something I can
never touch. When I touch
her shoulder she turns,
her damp cheek bathed
in the first soft light
of a day begun like
no other. She says
my name, one hushed
long syllable that means
I have entered again
the single presence she holds.

3.
Once, as a boy, I
climbed the attic stairs
in a sleeping house
and entered a room
no one used. I found
a trunk full of letters
and post cards from a man
who had travelled for years
and then come home to die.
In moonlight each one
said the same thing: how
long the nights were, how
cold it was so far away,
and how it had to end.

EACH TIME IS DIFFERENT

1.
The first death was difficult.
I sat alone in the corner of
my third grade classroom.
The others were gone, the teacher
would be back, she'd said, and I
must wait for her. I could hear
a bell tolling from St. Joseph's.
Their children would be going
soon, and maybe I would move
among them quietly, hoping to go
unnoticed. Down the long hall
I saw the old janitor lean
his wet mop against the wall;
a match flared in his face,
and then the whole world darkened.

2.
I stopped the car and left the motor
running, and the other two
asleep under a blanket in
the back seat. I pissed against
the gray, scarred trunk of a roadside
oak whose bare branches bowed
under the weight of last night's
new snow. Now it was dawn,
yellow and thin, crackling
the windshield. Off in the distance
I heard the sudden angry bite
of something like a rifle,
and then I saw him—one man
in a suit of long white underwear—
pushing the inner fire out
in sudden bursts, and the axe
rising and falling into
the long hull of a stricken tree.
His muttering too far to hear,
the charred fragments flying,
and all around him
the ground cluttered and stained.

3.

There had been a storm, low
gray clouds coming in, and the sea
the colour of wasted iron riding
up the shore to break over
the fishing boats. I walked
a while smelling nothing and tasting
the salt that crusted on lips
and eyes. Where was I going so early?
The wise world slept that day,
and one man searched the long
flat beach that stretched as far
as I could see, empty and steaming.
Out at sea, not even the gulls
to greet each blackened wave
that broke in sudden shouts
of foam. I began to sing quietly
at first, but that seemed far
too pointless, and so I shouted
for all I was worth, still unheard.

4.

A huge station, almost empty,
and a voice in a language no one
understood announcing cities that
never were, Babylon, Ninevah,
Flat Rock, What Cheer. There were
five of us, a woman in a blue coat
glistening with rain and four men
all at a great distance, and above
a clock that had stopped. A man
opened his paper and sighed, somewhere
there was a world, alive and rioting,
somewhere life as we had never
known it went on and on,
but we were here, waiting

because that was all we had
been brought here for, probably all
we were good for, and we were good.

5.
Some day soon, I'll go back
and stand under the dark tower
of that blackened church I passed
as a young man. What held it
up, I wondered every evening,
and I could almost feel the great
blocks of damaged granite
sliding toward me as the sky pressed
down on it from all sides.
I could hear the first sighs
and groans, as one hears a train
—miles off—in the tracks, stands
and moves back to give it passage.
I will look up and hear nothing
or feel a certain kinship with
a place so old, the cross still
carving a blackened sky, not
as a symbol of power or belief
but as a mark beneath which
something we made once lived and died.

THE LAST STEP

Once I was a small grain
of fire burning on the rim
of day, and I waited in silence
until the dawn released me
and I climbed into the light.
Here, in the brilliant orchard,
the thick-skinned oranges
doze in winter light,
late roses shred the wind,
and blood rains into
the meadows of winter grass.

I thought I would find my father
and hand in hand we would pace off
a child's life, I thought the air,
crystal around us, would hold
his words until they became
me, never to be forgotten.
I thought the rain was far off
under another sky. I thought
that to become a man I
had only to wait, and the years,
gathering slowly, would take me there.

They took me somewhere else.
The twisted fig tree, the almond,
not yet white crowned, the slow
tendrils of grape reaching
into the sky are companions
for a time, but nothing goes
the whole way. Not even the snail
smeared to death on a flat rock
or the tiny sparrow fallen from
the nest and flaring the yellow grass.
The last step, like an entrance,
is alone, in darkness, and without song.

THE FACE

A strange wind off the night.
I have come here to talk
to you at last, here
in an empty hotel room
half the world away from home.
Our tracks have crossed
how many times—a dozen
at least—and yet it's more
than forty years since I saw
you, solemn and hurt, gazing
from your favorite window
at the night that would
soon flood your eyes and darken
the living veins. Below,
the city is almost
asleep. An old man, no
taller than a boy, mumbles
drunkenly on his way,
and then only a sentry
passes from time to time,
his head sunk to his chest,
his eyes closed against
the strange summer cold.

We should all be asleep.
The hour is good for
nothing else, and yet
I cannot sleep because
suddenly today I caught
your presence beside me
on the street as I hadn't
before in all these years.
A tall man laid aside
his paper and stared at me,
a man no older than I,
with the long, sad face
that passed from you

to me. I kept walking,
feeling his eyes on me,
and when I turned at last
he was gone and the bench
filled with dirty children.
I went back—but no—
he was gone, and wherever
I walked I felt those eyes
on me and felt somehow
a time had come when
we might speak at last.

And so I do. I say, Father,
the years have brought
me here, still your son,
they have brought me
to a life I cannot
understand. I'm silent.
A ship is mooring
in the great harbor,
and the only voice
that comes back is the faint
after-ringing of my own.
I say, Father, the dark
moon above this battered city
must once have guided you
across the twelve frontiers
you crossed to save
your life. It leads me
nowhere, for I'm a free man,
alone as you were,
but going nowhere. I too
have lost my three sons
to America, I too have climbed
the long hillsides
of Spain in early light
as our forefathers did,

and gazed down at the sea,
deep and silent. I prayed
for some small hope
which never came. I know
the life you lost. I
have it here, Father,
where you left it, in
the long face of Spain,
in these hands, long
and broken like your own,
in the silence collecting
between each ringing
of my heart, the silence
you annoint me with each day.

Below, the sentry passes
once more in a new light,
for morning is graying
the streets of this quarter.
He wipes his nose on
the rough green wool
of his sleeve and stamps
his feet. Spain will waken
soon to street cries, to
the cries of children,
the cries of the lost men
and women of Barcelona
naming their despair.
I will walk among them,
tired and useless. Today
I will not talk, not
even to myself, for
it is time to listen,
as though some secret
message came blaring
over the megaphones,
or a voice mumbled below

the waves of traffic, as though
one word mattered more
than another in this world,
in this city, broken and stained,
which is the home of no one,
though it shouts out all
our names. I will listen
as though you spoke and told
me all you never knew
of why the earth takes
back all she gives and
even that comes to be enough.

III

LET ME BEGIN AGAIN

Let me begin again as a speck
of dust caught in the night winds
sweeping out to sea. Let me begin
this time knowing the world is
salt water and dark clouds, the world
is grinding and sighing all night, and dawn
comes slowly and changes nothing. Let
me go back to land after a lifetime
of going nowhere. This time lodged
in the feathers of some scavenging gull
white above the black ship that docks
and broods upon the oily waters of
your harbor. This leaking freighter
has brought a hold full of hayforks
from Spain, great jeroboams of dark
Algerian wine and quill pens that can't
write English. The sailors have stumbled
off toward the bars or the bright houses.
The captain closes his log and falls asleep.
1/10'28. Tonight I shall enter my life
after being at sea for ages, quietly,
in a hospital named for an automobile.
The one child of millions of children
who has flown alone by the stars
above the black wastes of moonless waters
that stretched forever, who has turned
golden in the full sun of a new day.
A tiny wise child who this time will love
his life because it is like no other.

SNOW

Today the snow is drifting
on Belle Isle, and the ducks
are searching for some opening
to the filthy waters of their river.
On Grand River Avenue, which is not
in Venice but in Detroit, Michigan,
the traffic has slowed to a standstill
and yet a sober man has hit a parked car
and swears to the police he was
not guilty. The bright squads of children
on their way to school howl
at the foolishness of the world
they will try not to inherit.
Seen from inside a window,
even a filthy one like those
at Automotive Supply Company, the snow
which has been falling for hours
is more beautiful than even the spring
grass which once unfurled here
before the invention of steel and fire,
for spring grass is what the earth sang
in answer to the new sun, to
melting snow, and the dark rain
of spring nights. But snow is nothing.
It has no melody or form, it
is as though the tears of all
the lost souls rose to heaven
and were finally heard and blessed
with substance and the power of flight
and given their choice chose then
to return to earth, to lay their
great pale cheek against the burning
cheek of earth and say, There, there, child.

DAWN, 1952

1.

Dawn. 1952. Late in the year.
The man I was chosen to be
wakens early as he always does
even on the morning of the day he died.
He stares into the darkness, the men
are all asleep except for him, and he
hears them around him breathing
and thrashing, and wonders, Why here
in this Korea against a people
we had never heard of? He wishes
he could cry, put his head between
his hands and rock forward and let
the tears held back for so long
stream between his fingers. He wishes
his life had somehow been another's,
someone tired and bored, rising
for work in a cold apartment
this morning on Chicago Boulevard
across from the barred forbidden seminary.

2.

But I said, No, no, I will not go, and
they let me go, knowing I was nothing.
I did cry. I put my hands between
my legs, alone, in the room I came
to love because it was all the room
I had, and pitched forward and cried
without hope or relief, for myself
and for all the others who haunted me
half the world away from their going.
I could still walk the streets of
this city, and there might be children
in the day's last light asking for coins,
there might be trains heading for
other towns or pulling the tanks
and half-tracks destined for that war.

In a bar somewhere there might be
the woman who'd say, Everyone loses,
and put her arm around me for no reason.
I wanted to die in flames and be reborn.

3.
I cannot now remember the flames
except those of the great forge room
where the burning metals pressed me
down into a silence deeper than still water.
The men around me quieted long before
dawn and worked on with sudden gasps
of breath crying out even over the roar
of the huge descending presses. I can
remember the little fire of paper and scraps
in a bleached-out oil drum in the snow
on the shoulder of US 24 where we
stamped our feet and took the day's
first drink even before the day had
come leaking one flaring match at
a time. Suddenly the shapes of men,
parked cars, the long road stretching
to another state south of us, a world
no one hoped for was here on
a cold day in late 1952. And if
it was work you wanted, there was
plenty of it to get you through the day.

DARK HEAD

Wakened suddenly by
my own voice, I know
I've said your name,
and you stir, your breath
as sweet as milk, and give
me first a hand to hold
and then your head to cradle.
How we came to be together
from the distant ends
of a continent, how we
gave first our hearts
and then the rest, I
can't say. The night is
ending, the dawn I once
prayed for is cracking
along the eastern rim
of hills, and the first light
floods this filthy valley
of the Ohio River. Here
and there a house puts on
a light, and someone
wakens to a life as strong
as the smell of urine
in the broken cellars
of the houses I walk by
each day. Once more you
are sleeping in my arms,
the arms of a man
you don't know yet trust.
I'm alone, and more,
awake to the life
that tears us apart,
content to see the day
come on flaming window
after window. Today
I shall be gone and you
will be alone again. Today

or tomorrow I shall be fire,
then ashes, then a hint
of something animal
moving out of the corners
of the wind, and then at last
I shall be nothing, not
even the echo of someone's
voice, and then I'll be
ourselves once more,
this world, opening
in each eye and damp fist
for those who would have her.

NOW IT CAN BE TOLD

What would it mean to lose this life
and go wandering the hallways
of that house in search of another self?
Not knowing, I wore a little amulet
to keep the evil from my heart, and yet
when the Day of Atonement came I did not
bow my head or bind myself at wrist and brow
because I knew I would atone. Silently
I would become all the small deaths
which gave me this one life.
I told this to the woman who loved
me more than life, and she wept
inconsolably, and thus I learned we
must love nothing more than life,
for when I am gone who will she
take her one loss to? Will she know
that somewhere close, perhaps in
the glow of old wood or in the frost
that glistens on the ripening orange,
is the grist and sweat of the one she loved?
Curse the sky. All it can answer
with is rain or snow. Curse
the sun, and perhaps the dead moon
will dawn tomorrow on a planet
equally dead. I am ready. I walk
the paths the children made, under
the canopy of branches and heavy leaves,
I find small tunnels where I could
find warmth and silence for a century.
In the high grasses of mountain meadows,
though it is marshy underfoot, I could
come to rest even in wind. Perhaps
a thousand years from now, a lost
boy or girl will catch the sight
of the bronze star that fortunately
saved me from nothing, and as he
stoops to untangle the blackened chain

he will have bowed his head the one time
I could not. He will raise the last
persistent portion of me and under a clear
sky wonder at its meaning, and let it
fall back to rest. Now it can be told:
I lived wisely, in the sight of everything,
and told no one how to live, and one day
after the spring rains I helped a child
find his way. If there are tears, they
should be tears of joy, for I am found
who was lost, and once more I've come back
to this earth, smudged and clouded with
a child's wonder. Warmed, close to life,
though dull and ancient, I still gleam,
like worn cloth, not like a woman's eyes.

WORDS

Another dawn, leaden
and cold. I am up
alone, searching
again for words
that will make
some difference
and finding none,
or rather finding these
who do not
make a difference.
I hear my son
waking for work—
he is late and doesn't
have time for coffee
or *hello*. The door
closes, a motor
turns over, and once
more it's only
me and the gray day.

Lately I've been
running by day,
drinking by night,
as though first to build
a man and then destroy
him—this for
three months, and
I don't find it foolish
—a man almost 50
who still knows so
little of why he's
alive and would turn
away from answers,
turn to the blankness
that follows my nights
or the pounding of
the breath, the sweat

oiling every part
of me, running
even from my hair.

I want to rise above
nothing, not even you.
I want to love women
until the love burns
me alive. I want
to rock God's daughter
until together we
become one wave
of the sea that brought
us into being. I
want your blessing,
whoever you are who
has the power to give
me a name for
whatever I am. I want
you to lead me to
the place within me
where I am every
man and woman, the trees
floating in the cold haze
of January, the small
beasts whose names
I have forgotten, the ache
I feel to be no
longer only myself.

Tonight my son
will come home, his
hands swollen and cracked,
his face gray with
exhaustion. He will
slump before his dinner
and eat. He will say

nothing of how much
it costs to be 18
and tear some small
living for yourself
with only your two hands.
My wife will say nothing
of the helplessness
she feels seeing her
men rocking on
their separate seas.
We are three people
bowing our heads to
all she has given us,
to bread and wine and meat.
The windows have gone
dark, but the room is
quiet in yellow light.
Nothing needs to be said.

YOU CAN HAVE IT

My brother comes home from work
and climbs the stairs to our room.
I can hear the bed groan and his shoes drop
one by one. You can have it, he says.

The moonlight streams in the window
and his unshaven face is whitened
like the face of the moon. He will sleep
long after noon and waken to find me gone.

Thirty years will pass before I remember
that moment when suddenly I knew each man
has one brother who dies when he sleeps
and sleeps when he rises to face this life,

and that together they are only one man
sharing a heart that always labors, hands
yellowed and cracked, a mouth that gasps
for breath and asks, Am I gonna make it?

All night at the ice plant he had fed
the chute its silvery blocks, and then I
stacked cases of orange soda for the children
of Kentucky, one gray box-car at a time

with always two more waiting. We were twenty
for such a short time and always in
the wrong clothes, crusted with dirt
and sweat. I think now we were never twenty.

In 1948 in the city of Detroit, founded
by de la Mothe Cadillac for the distant purposes
of Henry Ford, no one wakened or died,
no one walked the streets or stoked a furnace,

for there was no such year, and now
that year has fallen off all the old newspapers,
calendars, doctors' appointments, bonds,
wedding certificates, drivers licenses.

The city slept. The snow turned to ice.
The ice to standing pools or rivers
racing in the gutters. Then bright grass rose
between the thousands of cracked squares,

and that grass died. I give you back 1948.
I give you all the years from then
to the coming one. Give me back the moon
with its frail light falling across a face.

Give me back my young brother, hard
and furious, with wide shoulders and a curse
for God and burning eyes that look upon
all creation and say, You can have it.

When I was first born
the world was another place.
Men were somehow taller
and sang a great deal. I sang
as soon as I could. I sang
to the roads I drove over.
I sang to the winds, and I loved
them. It seemed I loved
so much that at times I
shook like a leaf
the moment before it surrenders
the branch and takes the air.
Little wonder I aged so fast,
and before I was forty
I was wizened and tiny, shrunken
like my Grandpa, and like him
afraid of nothing. I think
I would have died early
had I not been re-born
American, blue-eyed, tall.
This time I smoked Luckys,
let my hair grow long,
and never prayed. Except
for the smoking people said
I was like Jesus, except
for that and not knowing
the answers to anything. This
time too I drove badly because
my head was always filled
with tunes and words, and when
the songs went wild, so did I.
Four times I was arressted
for drunk driving, and the police
could not understand a man
so full of joy and empty
of drugs and alcohol. They
would make me walk a line,

but instead I danced and sang
like a lunatic. Yes,
even alone at night, blinded
by their headlights and pushed
by rough unseen hands,
I knew that life was somehow
all I would be given
and it was more than enough.
The months in jail were nothing—
my children came on weekends,
and they seemed proud of me,
though each week I grew
more tiny and tired. They
thought I was happy.
In the soft work shirt and
pale jeans, I was once more
the father of their infancies.
My wife's tears fell burning
my hands, for to her
there was something magical
about me, something that
could not survive the harsh voices,
the bars, the armed men. I died
in her eyes. I could feel
the pain of that death
like a fever coming over me,
rising along my back, up
through my neck and descending
into my eyes like blindness.
This time I died altogether,
without a word, and all
the separate atoms that held
my name scattered into
the mouths of bus conductors
and television repairmen.
I could have lived one
more time as so many

dollars and cents, but given
the choice I asked to remain
nothing. So now I am
a remembered ray of darkness
that catches at the corners
of your sight, a flat calm
in the oceans that never rest,
a yearning that rises
in your throat when you
least expect it, and screams
in a voice no one understands,
Let me be!
Let me be!

7 YEARS FROM SOMEWHERE

The highway ended
and we got out and walked
to where the bridge
had washed out and stared
down at the river moving
but clear to the bottom
of dark rocks. We
wondered, can we go back
and to what? In the hills
of the lower Atlas
7 years ago. You
pointed to a tall shepherd
racing along the crest
of a green hill, and
then there were four,
and they came down, stood
before us, dirty, green
eyed Berbers, their faces
open and laughing. One
took my hand and stroked
the soft white palm
with fingers as brown
and hard as wood. The sun
was beginning to drop
below the peaks, and I
said *Fez*, and they
answered in a language
we hadn't heard before.
Fez, and with gestures
of a man swimming
one told us to double
back, and we would find
a bridge. We left them
standing together in their
long robes, waving and laughing,
and went on to Fez, Meknes,
Tetuan, Ceuta, Spain,

Paris, here. I have
been lost since, wandering
in a bombed-out American
city among strangers
who meant me no harm.
Moving from the bars
to the streets, and coming
home alone to talk
to no one or myself
until the first light
broke the sky and I could
sleep a moment and waken
in the world we made
and will never call
ours, to waken to
the smell of bourbon
and sweat and another day
with no bridge, no old city
cupped carefully in
a bowl of mountains,
no one to take this hand,
the five perfect fingers
of the soul, and hold it
as one holds a blue egg
found in tall grasses
and smile and say something
that means nothing, that
means you are, you
are, and you are home.

Philip Levine was born in 1928 in Detroit and was formally educated there, at the public schools and at Wayne University. After a succession of stupid jobs he left the city for good, living in various parts of the country before he settled in Fresno, California, where he now teaches. His books include *On the Edge* (1963), *Not This Pig* (1968), *Pili's Wall* (1971), *Red Dust* (1971), *They Feed They Lion* (1972), *1933* (1974), *The Names of the Lost* (1976) and *Ashes, Poems Old and New* (1979).